THIS LAND CALLED AMERICA: **MISSOURI**

CREATIVE EDUCATION

Published by Creative Education
P.O. Box 227, Mankato, Minnesota 56002
Creative Education is an imprint of The Creative Company
www.thecreativecompany.us

Book and cover design by Blue Design (www.bluedes.com)
Art direction by Rita Marshall
Printed in the United States of America

Photographs by Corbis (Bettmann, Walter Bibikow/JAI, Dave G.
Houser, Lake County Museum, David Muench, Eric Nguyen, Connie
Ricca, Richard Hamilton Smith), Getty Images (Michael L. Abramson//
Time Life Pictures, Altrendo Nature, Hulton Archive, Tony Metaxas, Er-
nest H. Mills, MPI, Nick Vedros & Assoc., Panoramic Images, Donovan
Reese, Stock Montage, Art Wolfe)

Library of Congress Cataloging-in-Publication Data
Wimmer, Teresa.
Missouri / by Teresa Wimmer.
p. cm. — (This land called America)
Includes bibliographical references and index.
ISBN 978-1-58341-650-1
1. Missouri—Juvenile literature. I. Title. II. Series.
F466.3.W56 2008
977.8—dc22   2007015016

First Edition
9 8 7 6 5 4 3 2 1

This Land Called America

MISSOURI

Teresa Wimmer

Missouri

TERESA WIMMER

ON A MISTY SUMMER MORNING, TWO BOATERS FLOAT DOWN MISSOURI'S WINDING OSAGE RIVER. ONCE THE RIVER EMPTIES INTO LAKE OF THE OZARKS, A JET SKIER SPEEDS PAST THEM. SUDDENLY, THE EASYGOING BOATERS POWER UP THEIR MOTOR AND PURSUE THE JET SKIER. THEY ARE IN THE MOOD FOR A RACE. LATER, THEY DRIFT INTO A COOL CAVE. DRIPPING WATER HAS MADE INTRICATE DESIGNS ON THE CAVE'S WALLS. THE WALLS LOOK LIKE WATERFALLS OF YELLOW, GRAY, AND WHITE THAT HAVE TURNED TO STONE. WHEN THE BOATERS LEAVE THE CAVE, THEY CANNOT WAIT TO EXPLORE THE REST OF MISSOURI.

YEAR
1673   Louis Jolliet and Jacques Marquette become the first white men to set foot in Missouri.
EVENT

Gateway to the West

About 2,000 years ago, people called Cahokians lived in Missouri. They built great earthen mounds for graves and ceremonies. They traveled in canoes up and down the Mississippi River to trade salt, corn, and stone tools for copper, seashells, and sharks' teeth from other lands.

Later, many other Indian tribes such as the Osage, Peoria, Shawnee, and Fox hunted, fished, and grew crops in Missouri's rich land and waters. The biggest tribe was the Osage. They lived in cone-shaped huts and hunted deer, elk, buffalo, and bears. The Osage women planted corn, beans, and pumpkins. The Osage were an imposing people, many standing taller than six feet (1.8 m).

In 1673, Canadian Louis Jolliet and Frenchman Jacques Marquette canoed down the Mississippi River to Missouri. There, they met the friendly Peoria Indians and saw the plentiful wildlife and green land. Soon afterward, French explorer René-Robert de La Salle claimed the area for France in 1682.

Many America Indians such as the Osage (above) hunted big animals such as buffalo for food (opposite).

YEAR

1735   The French establish the first permanent settlement at Ste. Genevieve.

EVENT

- 7 -

An important part of Missouri's history, Fort Osage has been rebuilt to show how it looked in the 1800s.

The first school opens in St. Louis, Missouri, and operates for the next 40 years.

The French set up trading posts in Missouri. Trappers caught beavers, muskrats, and otters. Then they traded the animals' furs with the Indians or shipped them to the eastern United States and to Europe. In 1764, French fur traders founded the village of St. Louis. That village later grew to become Missouri's largest city.

In 1803, France sold the Louisiana Territory to the U.S. for $15 million. The territory included Missouri and lands to its south, north, and west. President Thomas Jefferson wanted to learn more about Missouri and the rest of the territory he had just purchased.

The next year, Meriwether Lewis and William Clark set out from St. Louis to explore the new land. They brought back exciting news of the abundant natural resources, wildlife, and waters they found. Many people headed to Missouri to organize the villages and trading posts into cities and towns.

Soon, Missouri asked the U.S. government to make it a state. But the government did not know whether Missouri should be a free state or a slave state. Many people in Missouri owned slaves, but others wanted everyone in the state to be free. In the Missouri Compromise of 1820, the government decided to admit Maine as a free state in 1820 and Missouri as a slave state in 1821.

Steamboats were important to developing cities, such as St. Louis, along Missouri's rivers.

By the mid-1800s, people from the East had heard about gold in the mountains west of Missouri. They traveled in covered wagons and on horseback to find it. Some just passed through Missouri, but others stayed and made their homes there. They farmed the land and raised cattle. Kansas City became the center of the state's livestock and grain market.

During the American Civil War of 1861–1865, some Missourians fought for the North; others fought for the South. After the war, Missouri's slaves were freed and many immigrants from Ireland, Germany, Italy, and Czechoslovakia moved to its cities and farms. They lived in small houses made of logs or limestone and worked in lumber mills, flour mills, and other businesses.

Soon, schools and colleges were founded. Factories sprang up that made steamboat engines, lead pipe, textiles, and beer. New railroads carried Missouri bacon, beef, corn, oats, and apples to other parts of the country. Missouri was taking its place as an American manufacturing and farming leader.

YEAR

1817 — The *Zebulon Pike* becomes the first steamboat to travel up the Mississippi River to St. Louis.

EVENT

Welcome to
KANSAS CITY STOCKYARDS
AUCTION CENTER

In the Middle

MISSOURI HAS MORE STATES AS NEIGHBORS THAN ANY STATE EXCEPT TENNESSEE. TO THE NORTH IS IOWA. ON THE EASTERN SIDE ARE ILLINOIS, KENTUCKY, AND TENNESSEE. ARKANSAS IS MISSOURI'S SOUTHERN NEIGHBOR, AND OKLAHOMA AND KANSAS BORDER THE STATE ON THE WEST.

Four different land areas make up Missouri. The northwestern part was formed thousands of years ago by huge sheets of ice called glaciers. When the glaciers moved on, they left rolling hills and plains. Farms growing green and golden crops such as corn, soybeans, and wheat blanket the land.

The mighty Missouri River sweeps across the northern part of the state. South of the river, the rugged land is marked by cliffs and ridges made of rocks such as limestone and shale. Oak and maple trees and short, reddish grasses line the ridges. Deer, squirrels, and wild turkeys roam the forests. Purple coneflowers, red cardinal flowers, and violets dot the hillsides with color.

The Ozark Plateau makes up most of south-central Missouri. The land there is rocky and full of streams, lakes, and woods. Trout and other fish swim in the cool waters. Beavers, muskrats, and otters live in the woods and streams. When early explorers looked for silver in the Ozarks' hills, they did not find any. But they did find lead. Today, the Ozarks produce most of the country's lead supply.

Wild turkeys (above) forage for food such as grass in Missouri's cow pastures (opposite) and for nuts and berries in the forests.

YEAR

1847   St. Louis is connected to the East Coast by telegraph for the first time.

EVENT

Rivers flowing downward through the Ozarks have cut deep river canyons. The sand, water, and stones of a river carve into the soft limestone hills. The hills at Johnson's Shut-Ins State Park are especially smooth. People can slide down the scooped-out hills, even without using inner tubes.

The hills are also filled with many caves. Bats live in some of them. In other caves, water dripping from the rock produces long, pointed forms called stalactites and stalagmites. Some of them look like frozen waterfalls or twisted spaghetti.

In the northern Ozarks is the Lake of the Ozarks region. Lake of the Ozarks is one of the largest man-made lakes in

Blanchard Springs Caverns (above) are part of a cave system that runs underneath the Ozarks, the mountains that feature Taum Sauk (opposite).

1873   Educator Susan Blow starts the nation's first kindergarten in St. Louis.

Some of the forested land in Missouri's Ozarks was once owned by people who had mills and homes there.

America. In 1931, people created it by damming the Osage River. The lake is a popular spot for fishing, canoeing, and boating. Nearby is Taum Sauk Mountain. At 1,772 feet (540 m), it is the highest point in Missouri.

In the spring, Missouri's rivers and lakes often flood. Melting snow from western mountains and northern lands flows into the Missouri and Mississippi rivers. Sometimes, whole towns can be washed away. During the Great Flood of 1993, 112 of the state's 114 counties were declared disaster areas. The capital of Jefferson City lay beneath muddy floodwaters for most of the spring and summer.

Tornadoes often cause great damage in Missouri, too. The state lies in an area of the country called "Tornado Alley." On average, more than 50 tornadoes plow through the state each year. In 1925, a devastating tornado passed through Missouri, Illinois, and Indiana. Hundreds of people were killed, and many buildings and crops were destroyed.

Summers in Missouri can be very hot and humid. Winters are cold, with average temperatures of 33 °F (.6 °C). Snow does fall there, but usually not more than a few inches each winter. Most of the state receives about 40 inches (102 cm) of rain each year.

Most tornadoes occur in the United States, but they have been seen on every continent except Antarctica.

YEAR

1875   A grasshopper plague causes millions of dollars in damage to Missouri's crops.

EVENT

- 17 -

Working and Playing

Because Missouri sits in the center of the U.S., it is an important hub for manufacturing, warehousing, and transportation. Most of the state's population lives around either St. Louis or Kansas City. But farming is as important today as it ever was.

The first Europeans to settle in Missouri were French. They built the first permanent settlement at Ste. Genevieve around 1735. In the mid-1800s, Germans came to Missouri. They farmed and grew fruits such as grapes and apples. Later, Italians came to the St. Louis area. They worked in brick factories or mined for lead, clay, and coal.

In 1835, Samuel Clemens (also known as Mark Twain) was born in Florida, Missouri, but soon moved to Hannibal. When he got older, he traveled the Mississippi River as a steamboat pilot and mined for silver in the Nevada mountains. Then he started writing books based on his Missouri childhood. In

Although he never worked in a Missouri factory or warehouse (opposite), famous novelist Mark Twain (above) did have many other odd jobs.

Robert Ford claimed a $10,000 reward when he shot an unarmed Jesse James (pictured) in 1882.

1876, *The Adventures of Tom Sawyer* was published, and *The Adventures of Huckleberry Finn* followed in 1884. They are considered classics of American literature.

In the early days of statehood, Missouri was a wild frontier. The outlaw Jesse James was born in Clay County in 1847. He later led a gang that robbed many banks and trains across the Midwest. At one point, Missouri's governor offered a lot of money for James's capture. In 1882, a member of the James gang shot and killed Jesse. After James's death, the gang disbanded.

Missourians are always looking for ways to improve farming. In 1864, George Washington Carver was born to slaves on a farm near Diamond Grove. As a child, Carver loved to garden and grow plants. Later, he worked as an agricultural researcher at Tuskegee Institute in Alabama. He showed Southern farmers how to grow peanuts, sweet potatoes, and other crops to make the soil richer. He became an expert on making cheese, soap, and milk from peanuts.

Today, many of Missouri's small farms of the past are gone. Big, corporate farms have taken their place. Farmers raise cattle, chickens, and hogs. They grow corn, soybeans, and wheat.

YEAR
1917 The present Missouri State Capitol, in Jefferson City, is completed.
EVENT

The Osage River is dammed, creating Lake of the Ozarks.

People called biotechnologists work with plants in laboratories at Monsanto Company.

Much of the state's livestock is processed in Kansas City.

Today, 85 percent of Missourians are white. African Americans make up the next largest group, at 11.5 percent. Some Hispanics and Native Americans also live there. Recently, Asian immigrants from Thailand, Laos, and the Philippines have come to St. Louis. Many of them work in factories or own bakeries, restaurants, or grocery stores.

In the Anheuser-Busch brewing house, grains such as barley are made into alcohol.

Many Missourians work for major corporations. Hallmark Cards, Inc. in Kansas City produces greeting cards. In St. Louis, many people make pet food at Ralston Purina. Others make beer at Anheuser-Busch, Inc. Monsanto Company is an important agricultural research company. People there work to develop different varieties of crops.

YEAR

1951   The Missouri River floods and destroys Kansas City's meat-packing warehouses.

EVENT

- 23 -

"Show Me" Missouri

McDonnell Douglas F-4 factory

O ther people in cities work in stores, hospitals, schools, and banks. Electronics, automobile, and airplane industries employ many people, too. Because more people are moving to the cities, construction jobs in Kansas City and elsewhere have become more plentiful.

The Ozark region has a long history of storytelling. But Missourians take pride in not believing everything they are told. They do not say, "Tell me"; they say, "Show me." That is one explanation for why Missouri is nicknamed the "Show Me State."

Children whose parents or grandparents may have come from Asian countries can do well in Missouri's schools (above); F-4 Phantom jets (opposite) were made at a St. Louis factory.

1965   The Gateway Arch, designed by architect Eero Saarinen, is completed in St. Louis.

Show Me Missouri

MISSOURI HAS LONG BEEN THE "GATEWAY TO THE WEST." THE CITY OF INDEPENDENCE WAS THE STARTING POINT FOR THE OREGON, CALIFORNIA, AND SANTA FE TRAILS. IN THE 1800S, MANY PIONEER SETTLERS FOLLOWED THESE TRAILS WEST TO FIND RICHES AND LAND.

Nothing represents this "gateway" state better than the Gateway Arch. It stands at the edge of the Mississippi River and towers over St. Louis. The Arch is 630 feet (192 m) of curved, brilliant steel. In a small capsule that works like an elevator, visitors can be pulled to the top of the arch and look out at the tiny buildings below.

St. Louis hosted the World's Fair in 1904, when it celebrated the 100th anniversary of the Louisiana Purchase. The fair featured huge palaces filled with new products and innovations that people could expect to see in the future. For the first time, people also tasted foods such as ice cream cones and iced tea.

Missourians have always loved their music. Each June, Sedalia hosts the Scott Joplin Ragtime Festival. The festival was named for one of the first famous black musicians in America. Visitors can eat tasty food, learn more about Joplin—who studied music in Sedalia—and listen to lots of toe-tapping ragtime music.

The biggest earthquake ever recorded in the continental U.S. shook New Madrid, Missouri, in February 1812. This was the third quake the town had experienced in two months.

The Gateway Arch (opposite) was built 61 years after the events of the World's Fair (above) helped St. Louis gain national attention.

New Madrid lies on a fault line, and sometimes the land on both sides of the fault line moves. Scientists expect another big earthquake to strike the area in the future.

In the days before the U.S. Postal Service, the Pony Express picked up and delivered people's mail. Riders on horseback left St. Joseph with their mailbags bound for California. Now, visitors can walk through a museum celebrating the Pony Express. They can choose their own horse, send a telegraph message, and see and hear what the original riders did.

On a hot day in nearby Kansas City, people can run through one of the city's many water fountains. Kansas Citians boast that their city has more fountains than any city in the world except for Rome, Italy.

Country music floats through the air in the town of Branson. Nestled in the Ozarks, the small town's country-western theaters provide live entertainment to millions of visitors each year. Nearby Silver Dollar City has been turned from an old mining town into a big amusement park. Visitors love shooting down one of the many waterslides or riding the roller coasters.

In addition to enjoying a variety of outdoor activities, Missourians also love their professional sports. The state's

YEAR
1977   Gwen B. Giles becomes Missouri's first female African American state senator.
EVENT

In October 2006, at Busch Stadium, the St. Louis Cardinals won their 10th World Series title.

Missouri governor Mel Carnahan dies in a plane crash just outside St. Louis.

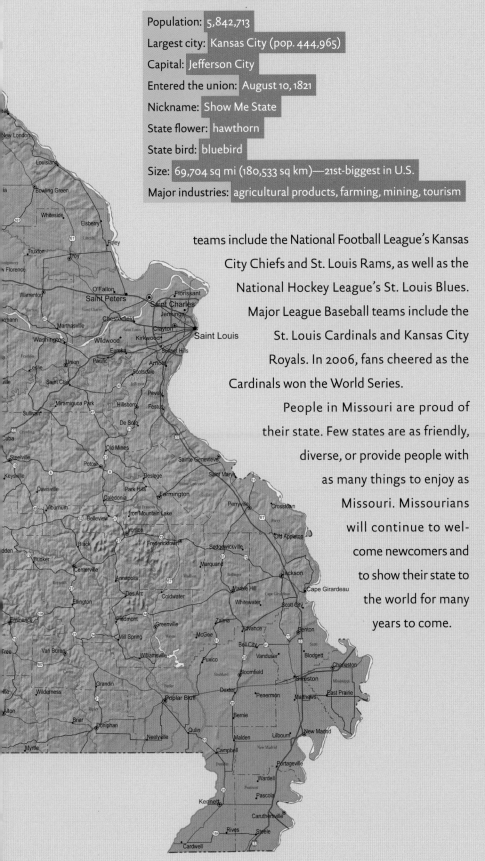

QUICK FACTS

Population: 5,842,713

Largest city: Kansas City (pop. 444,965)

Capital: Jefferson City

Entered the union: August 10, 1821

Nickname: Show Me State

State flower: hawthorn

State bird: bluebird

Size: 69,704 sq mi (180,533 sq km)—21st-biggest in U.S.

Major industries: agricultural products, farming, mining, tourism

teams include the National Football League's Kansas City Chiefs and St. Louis Rams, as well as the National Hockey League's St. Louis Blues. Major League Baseball teams include the St. Louis Cardinals and Kansas City Royals. In 2006, fans cheered as the Cardinals won the World Series.

People in Missouri are proud of their state. Few states are as friendly, diverse, or provide people with as many things to enjoy as Missouri. Missourians will continue to welcome newcomers and to show their state to the world for many years to come.

BIBLIOGRAPHY

Bennett, Michelle. *Missouri*. New York: Benchmark Books, 2001.

Hintz, Martin. *Missouri*. New York: Children's Press, 1999.

Missouri Division of Tourism. "Welcome to Missouri." VisitMO.com. http://www.visitmo.com/.

Missouri Secretary of State. "All About Missouri History." Missouri State Government. http://www.sos.mo.gov/archives/history/.

Nagel, Paul C. *Missouri: A History*. Lawrence, Kansas: University Press of Kansas, 1989.

State Historical Society of Missouri. "Famous Missourians." State of Missouri. http://www.umsystem.edu/shs/famousmissourians/.

INDEX

American Indians 6–7, 23
  Cahokians 6
  Osage tribe 7
animals 7, 9, 10, 13, 20
border states 12
Branson 28
Carver, George Washington 20
Clemens, Samuel *see* Twain, Mark
French explorers 7
fur traders 9
industries 10, 13, 18, 19, 20, 23–24
  farming 10, 13, 18, 19, 20
  major businesses 23–24
  manufacturing 10, 18, 19, 23
  mining 19
James, Jesse 20
Jefferson City 17
Johnson's Shut-Ins State Park 14
Kansas City 10, 18, 23, 24, 28
land regions and features 5, 6, 13–14, 17, 19, 24, 28
  caves 5, 14
  highest point 17
  lakes and rivers 5, 6, 13, 14, 17, 19

  mountains 17
  Ozarks 13, 14, 24, 28
  plains 13
Lewis and Clark expedition 9
Missouri Compromise 9
museums 28
natural disasters 17, 27–28
natural resources 9, 13
plants 13
population 10, 19, 23
  countries represented 10, 19, 23
recreational activities 5, 14, 17, 28
Scott Joplin Ragtime Festival 27
sports 28, 31
  professional teams 28, 31
St. Louis 9, 18, 23, 27
  1904 World's Fair 27
  Gateway Arch 27
state nicknames 24, 26
statehood 9, 20
Twain, Mark 19–20
weather and climate 17